Personal Quilt Registry

The Personal Registry of _____

American Quilter's Society

P. O. Box 3290 ● Paducah, Kentucky 42001

This handy registry is an invaluable aid to every quilter, dealer, collector and investor. Not only will it serve as a perfect insurance record in case of fire or theft, but will also be treasured by you and your family for years to come. For the Quilter it will add satisfaction and joy to the project. For the dealer and investor it will provide accurate information for business and tax records. (May we suggest a different book for each type of quilting project, i.e., wall hangings, pattern blocks, quilts, clothing, etc.)

Additional copies of this book may be obtained from
a chapter member of The American Quilter's Society,
your favorite bookseller, sewing center or fabric shop,

Or From:
THE AMERICAN QUILTER'S SOCIETY
P. O. Box 3290
Paducah, Kentucky 42001

@$3.95 per copy. When ordering by mail, please
add $1.00 to cover postage and handling.

Copyright: American Quilter's Society, 1984

This book or any part thereof may not be reproduced without
the written consent of the American Quilter's Society.

Master Index

Project	Pages

PHOTO

Item _____

Pattern _____ Size _____

Color Scheme _____

Reference _____

Fabrics & Yardage _____

_____

_____

Completed Cost _____

Date Started _____ Completed _____

Cont'd on next page

Page (   )

Constructed By _____

Quilted By _____

Appraised By _____ Value _____

Updated Appraisals _____ , _____ ; _____ , _____ ; _____ , _____ .
　　　　　　　　　　　Date　　Amount　　Date　　Amount　　Date　　Amount

Purpose of Project:

Gift _____
　　　　　　　　　　　　　Presented to

Sale _____
　　　　　　　　　　　　　Sold To

Personal Use _____
　　　　　　　　　　　　　Used For

Purchased Quilts

Purchased From _____

Address _____

Date Purchased _____Cost_____

Historical Information _____

_____

_____

_____

_____

_____

_____

_____

_____

Page (　　　)

Item _____

Pattern _____ Size _____

Color Scheme _____

Reference _____

Fabrics & Yardage _____

_____

_____

Completed Cost _____

Date Started _____ Completed _____

PHOTO

Cont'd on next page

Page (   )

Constructed By _____

Quilted By _____

Appraised By _____ Value _____

Updated Appraisals _____ , _____ ; _____ , _____ ; _____ , _____ .
                  Date   Amount   Date   Amount   Date   Amount

Purpose of Project:

Gift _____
                            Presented to

Sale _____
                            Sold To

Personal Use _____
                            Used For

Purchased Quilts

Purchased From _____

Address _____

Date Purchased _____Cost_____

Historical Information _____

_____

_____

_____

_____

_____

_____

_____

_____

PHOTO

Item _____

Pattern _____ Size _____

Color Scheme _____

Reference _____

Fabrics & Yardage _____

_____

_____

Completed Cost _____

Date Started _____ Completed _____

Cont'd on next page

Constructed By _____

Quilted By _____

Appraised By _____ Value _____

Updated Appraisals _____ , _____ ; _____ , _____ ; _____ , _____ .
                    Date   Amount   Date   Amount   Date   Amount

Purpose of Project:

Gift _____
                        Presented to

Sale _____
                          Sold To

Personal Use _____
                          Used For

Purchased Quilts

Purchased From _____

Address _____

Date Purchased _____Cost_____

Historical Information _____

_____

_____

_____

_____

_____

_____

_____

_____

Item _____

Pattern _____ Size _____

Color Scheme _____

Reference _____

Fabrics & Yardage _____

_____

_____

Completed Cost _____

Date Started _____ Completed _____

PHOTO

Cont'd on next page

Constructed By _____

Quilted By _____

Appraised By _____ Value _____

Updated Appraisals _____ , _____ ; _____ , _____ ; _____ , _____ .
                     Date   Amount   Date   Amount   Date   Amount

Purpose of Project:

Gift _____
                              Presented to

Sale _____
                              Sold To

Personal Use _____
                              Used For

Purchased Quilts

Purchased From _____

Address _____

Date Purchased _____Cost_____

Historical Information _____

_____

_____

_____

_____

_____

_____

_____

_____

PHOTO

Item _____

Pattern _____ Size _____

Color Scheme _____

Reference _____

Fabrics & Yardage _____

_____

_____

Completed Cost _____

Date Started _____ Completed _____

Cont'd on next page

Page (   )

Constructed By _____

Quilted By _____

Appraised By _____ Value _____

Updated Appraisals _____ , _____ ; _____ , _____ ; _____ , _____ .
                     Date   Amount   Date   Amount   Date   Amount

Purpose of Project:

Gift _____
                              Presented to

Sale _____
                                Sold To

Personal Use _____
                                Used For

Purchased Quilts

Purchased From _____

Address _____

Date Purchased _____Cost_____

Historical Information _____

_____

_____

_____

_____

_____

_____

_____

_____

Item _____

Pattern _____ Size _____

Color Scheme _____

Reference _____

Fabrics & Yardage _____

_____

_____

Completed Cost _____

Date Started _____ Completed _____

PHOTO

Cont'd on next page

Constructed By _____

Quilted By _____

Appraised By _____ Value _____

Updated Appraisals _____ , _____ ; _____ , _____ ; _____ , _____ .
                         Date   Amount   Date   Amount   Date   Amount

Purpose of Project:

Gift _____
                              Presented to

Sale _____
                              Sold To

Personal Use _____
                              Used For

Purchased Quilts

Purchased From _____

Address _____

Date Purchased _____Cost_____

Historical Information _____

_____

_____

_____

_____

_____

_____

_____

_____

PHOTO

Item _____

Pattern _____ Size _____

Color Scheme _____

Reference _____

Fabrics & Yardage _____

_____

_____

Completed Cost _____

Date Started _____ Completed _____

Cont'd on next page

Page (   )

Constructed By _____

Quilted By _____

Appraised By _____ Value _____

Updated Appraisals _____ , _____ ; _____ , _____ ; _____ , _____ .
                    Date   Amount   Date   Amount   Date   Amount

Purpose of Project:

Gift _____
                        Presented to

Sale _____
                        Sold To

Personal Use _____
                        Used For

Purchased Quilts

Purchased From _____

Address _____

Date Purchased _____Cost_____

Historical Information _____

_____

_____

_____

_____

_____

_____

_____

_____

Item _____

Pattern _____ Size _____

Color Scheme _____

Reference _____

Fabrics & Yardage _____

_____

_____

Completed Cost _____

Date Started _____ Completed _____

PHOTO

Cont'd on next page

Page (   )

Constructed By _____

Quilted By _____

Appraised By _____ Value _____

Updated Appraisals _____ , _____ ; _____ , _____ ; _____ , _____ .
                     Date   Amount   Date   Amount   Date   Amount

Purpose of Project:

Gift _____
                              Presented to

Sale _____
                              Sold To

Personal Use _____
                              Used For

Purchased Quilts

Purchased From _____

Address _____

Date Purchased _____Cost_____

Historical Information _____

_____

_____

_____

_____

_____

_____

_____

_____

PHOTO

Item _____

Pattern _____ Size _____

Color Scheme _____

Reference _____

Fabrics & Yardage _____

_____

_____

Completed Cost _____

Date Started _____ Completed _____

Cont'd on next page

Page (   )

Constructed By _____

Quilted By _____

Appraised By _____ Value _____

Updated Appraisals _____ , _____ ; _____ , _____ ; _____ , _____ .
                      Date   Amount   Date   Amount   Date   Amount

Purpose of Project:

Gift _____
                          Presented to

Sale _____
                          Sold To

Personal Use _____
                          Used For

Purchased Quilts

Purchased From _____

Address _____

Date Purchased _____Cost_____

Historical Information _____

_____

_____

_____

_____

_____

_____

_____

_____

Item _____

Pattern _____ Size _____

Color Scheme _____

Reference _____

Fabrics & Yardage _____

_____

_____

Completed Cost _____

Date Started _____ Completed _____

PHOTO

Cont'd on next page

Page (   )

Constructed By _____

Quilted By _____

Appraised By _____ Value _____

Updated Appraisals _____ , _____ ; _____ , _____ ; _____ , _____ .
 Date Amount Date Amount Date Amount

Purpose of Project:

Gift _____
 Presented to

Sale _____
 Sold To

Personal Use _____
 Used For

Purchased Quilts

Purchased From _____

Address _____

Date Purchased _____Cost_____

Historical Information _____

_____

_____

_____

_____

_____

_____

_____

_____

Page (   )

PHOTO

Item _____

Pattern _____ Size _____

Color Scheme _____

Reference _____

Fabrics & Yardage _____

_____

_____

Completed Cost _____

Date Started _____ Completed _____

Cont'd on next page

Page (   )

Constructed By _____

Quilted By _____

Appraised By _____ Value _____

Updated Appraisals _____ , _____ ; _____ , _____ ; _____ , _____ .
                    Date   Amount   Date   Amount   Date   Amount

Purpose of Project:

Gift _____
                    Presented to

Sale _____
                    Sold To

Personal Use _____
                    Used For

Purchased Quilts

Purchased From _____

Address _____

Date Purchased _____Cost_____

Historical Information _____

_____

_____

_____

_____

_____

_____

_____

Item _____

Pattern _____ Size _____

Color Scheme _____

Reference _____

Fabrics & Yardage _____

_____

_____

Completed Cost _____

Date Started _____ Completed _____

PHOTO

Cont'd on next page

Constructed By _____

Quilted By _____

Appraised By _____ Value _____

Updated Appraisals _____ , _____ ; _____ , _____ ; _____ , _____ .
                  Date   Amount   Date   Amount   Date   Amount

Purpose of Project:

Gift   _____
                        Presented to

Sale   _____
                        Sold To

Personal Use _____
                        Used For

Purchased Quilts

Purchased From _____

Address _____

Date Purchased _____Cost_____

Historical Information _____

_____

_____

_____

_____

_____

_____

_____

_____

PHOTO

Item _____

Pattern _____ Size _____

Color Scheme _____

Reference _____

Fabrics & Yardage _____

_____

_____

Completed Cost _____

Date Started _____ Completed _____

Cont'd on next page

Constructed By _____

Quilted By _____

Appraised By _____ Value _____

Updated Appraisals _____ , _____ ; _____ , _____ ; _____ , _____ .
                    Date   Amount   Date   Amount   Date   Amount

Purpose of Project:

Gift _____
                       Presented to

Sale _____
                       Sold To

Personal Use _____
                       Used For

Purchased Quilts

Purchased From _____

Address _____

Date Purchased _____Cost_____

Historical Information _____

_____

_____

_____

_____

_____

_____

_____

_____

Item _____

Pattern _____ Size _____

Color Scheme _____

Reference _____

Fabrics & Yardage _____

_____

_____

Completed Cost _____

Date Started _____ Completed _____

PHOTO

Cont'd on next page

Constructed By _____

Quilted By _____

Appraised By _____ Value _____

Updated Appraisals _____ , _____ ; _____ , _____ ; _____ , _____ .
                     Date   Amount   Date   Amount   Date   Amount

Purpose of Project:

Gift _____
                         Presented to

Sale _____
                         Sold To

Personal Use _____
                         Used For

Purchased Quilts

Purchased From _____

Address _____

Date Purchased _____Cost_____

Historical Information _____

_____

_____

_____

_____

_____

_____

_____

_____

Page (   )

PHOTO

Item _____

Pattern _____ Size _____

Color Scheme _____

Reference _____

Fabrics & Yardage _____

_____

_____

Completed Cost _____

Date Started _____ Completed _____

Cont'd on next page

Constructed By _____

Quilted By _____

Appraised By _____ Value _____

Updated Appraisals _____ , _____ ; _____ , _____ ; _____ , _____ .
                Date   Amount   Date   Amount   Date   Amount

Purpose of Project:

Gift _____
                       Presented to

Sale _____
                     Sold To

Personal Use _____
                     Used For

Purchased Quilts

Purchased From _____

Address _____

Date Purchased _____Cost_____

Historical Information _____

_____

_____

_____

_____

_____

_____

_____

Item _____

Pattern _____ Size _____

Color Scheme _____

Reference _____

Fabrics & Yardage _____

_____

_____

Completed Cost _____

Date Started _____ Completed _____

PHOTO

Cont'd on next page

Page (   )

Constructed By _____

Quilted By _____

Appraised By _____ Value _____

Updated Appraisals _____ , _____ ; _____ , _____ ; _____ , _____ .
                      Date   Amount   Date   Amount   Date   Amount

Purpose of Project:

Gift _____
                    Presented to

Sale _____
                    Sold To

Personal Use _____
                    Used For

Purchased Quilts

Purchased From _____

Address _____

Date Purchased _____Cost_____

Historical Information _____

_____

_____

_____

_____

_____

_____

_____

_____

PHOTO

Item _____

Pattern _____ Size _____

Color Scheme _____

Reference _____

Fabrics & Yardage _____

_____

_____

Completed Cost _____

Date Started _____ Completed _____

Cont'd on next page

Page (   )

Constructed By _____

Quilted By _____

Appraised By _____ Value _____

Updated Appraisals _____ , _____ ; _____ , _____ ; _____ , _____ .
                      Date   Amount   Date   Amount   Date   Amount

Purpose of Project:

Gift _____
                                    Presented to

Sale _____
                                    Sold To

Personal Use _____
                                    Used For

Purchased Quilts

Purchased From _____

Address _____

Date Purchased _____Cost_____

Historical Information _____

_____

_____

_____

_____

_____

_____

_____

_____

Page (   )

Item _____

Pattern _____ Size _____

Color Scheme _____

Reference _____

Fabrics & Yardage _____

_____

_____

Completed Cost _____

Date Started _____ Completed _____

PHOTO

Cont'd on next page

Page (   )

Constructed By _____

Quilted By _____

Appraised By _____ Value _____

Updated Appraisals _____ , _____ ; _____ , _____ ; _____ , _____ .
                     Date   Amount   Date   Amount   Date   Amount

Purpose of Project:

Gift _____
                           Presented to

Sale _____
                            Sold To

Personal Use _____
                            Used For

Purchased Quilts

Purchased From _____

Address _____

Date Purchased _____Cost_____

Historical Information _____

_____

_____

_____

_____

_____

_____

_____

_____

PHOTO

Item _____

Pattern _____ Size _____

Color Scheme _____

Reference _____

Fabrics & Yardage _____

_____

_____

Completed Cost _____

Date Started _____ Completed _____

Cont'd on next page

Constructed By _____

Quilted By _____

Appraised By _____ Value _____

Updated Appraisals _____ , _____ ; _____ , _____ ; _____ , _____ .
 Date Amount Date Amount Date Amount

Purpose of Project:

Gift _____
 Presented to

Sale _____
 Sold To

Personal Use _____
 Used For

Purchased Quilts

Purchased From _____

Address _____

Date Purchased _____Cost_____

Historical Information _____

_____

_____

_____

_____

_____

_____

_____

_____

Item _____

Pattern _____ Size _____

Color Scheme _____

Reference _____

Fabrics & Yardage _____

_____

_____

Completed Cost _____

Date Started _____ Completed _____

PHOTO

Cont'd on next page

Page (   )

Constructed By _____

Quilted By _____

Appraised By _____ Value _____

Updated Appraisals _____ , _____ ; _____ , _____ ; _____ , _____ .
                   Date   Amount   Date   Amount   Date   Amount

Purpose of Project:

Gift _____
                   Presented to

Sale _____
                   Sold To

Personal Use _____
                   Used For

Purchased Quilts

Purchased From _____

Address _____

Date Purchased _____Cost_____

Historical Information _____

_____

_____

_____

_____

_____

_____

_____

_____

PHOTO

Item _____

Pattern _____ Size _____

Color Scheme _____

Reference _____

Fabrics & Yardage _____

_____

_____

Completed Cost _____

Date Started _____ Completed _____

Cont'd on next page

Constructed By _____

Quilted By _____

Appraised By _____ Value _____

Updated Appraisals _____ , _____ ; _____ , _____ ; _____ , _____.
                    Date   Amount   Date   Amount   Date   Amount

Purpose of Project:

Gift _____
                          Presented to

Sale _____
                           Sold To

Personal Use _____
                            Used For

Purchased Quilts

Purchased From _____

Address _____

Date Purchased _____Cost_____

Historical Information _____

_____

_____

_____

_____

_____

_____

_____

_____

Page (   )

Item _____

Pattern _____ Size _____

Color Scheme _____

Reference _____

Fabrics & Yardage _____

_____

_____

Completed Cost _____

Date Started _____ Completed _____

PHOTO

Cont'd on next page

Constructed By _____

Quilted By _____

Appraised By _____ Value _____

Updated Appraisals _____ , _____ ; _____ , _____ ; _____ , _____.
 Date Amount Date Amount Date Amount

Purpose of Project:

Gift _____
 Presented to

Sale _____
 Sold To

Personal Use _____
 Used For

Purchased Quilts

Purchased From _____

Address _____

Date Purchased _____Cost_____

Historical Information _____

_____

_____

_____

_____

_____

_____

_____

_____

Page (   )

PHOTO

Item _____

Pattern _____ Size _____

Color Scheme _____

Reference _____

Fabrics & Yardage _____

_____

_____

Completed Cost _____

Date Started _____ Completed _____

Cont'd on next page

Page (   )

Constructed By _____

Quilted By _____

Appraised By _____ Value _____

Updated Appraisals _____ , _____ ; _____ , _____ ; _____ , _____.
$\qquad$ Date $\qquad$ Amount $\qquad$ Date $\qquad$ Amount $\qquad$ Date $\qquad$ Amount

Purpose of Project:

Gift _____
$\qquad$ Presented to

Sale _____
$\qquad$ Sold To

Personal Use _____
$\qquad$ Used For

Purchased Quilts

Purchased From _____

Address _____

Date Purchased _____Cost_____

Historical Information _____

_____

_____

_____

_____

_____

_____

_____

Item _____

Pattern _____ Size _____

Color Scheme _____

Reference _____

Fabrics & Yardage _____

_____

_____

Completed Cost _____

Date Started _____ Completed _____

PHOTO

Cont'd on next page

Constructed By _____

Quilted By _____

Appraised By _____ Value _____

Updated Appraisals _____ , _____ ; _____ , _____ ; _____ , _____ .
                           Date   Amount   Date   Amount   Date   Amount

Purpose of Project:

Gift _____
                             Presented to

Sale _____
                             Sold To

Personal Use _____
                             Used For

Purchased Quilts

Purchased From _____

Address _____

Date Purchased _____Cost_____

Historical Information _____

_____

_____

_____

_____

_____

_____

_____

_____

PHOTO

Item _____

Pattern _____ Size _____

Color Scheme _____

Reference _____

Fabrics & Yardage _____

_____

_____

Completed Cost _____

Date Started _____ Completed _____

Cont'd on next page

Page (   )

Constructed By _____

Quilted By _____

Appraised By _____ Value _____

Updated Appraisals _____ , _____ ; _____ , _____ ; _____ , _____ .
                    Date   Amount   Date   Amount   Date   Amount

Purpose of Project:

Gift _____
                              Presented to

Sale _____
                                Sold To

Personal Use _____
                                Used For

Purchased Quilts

Purchased From _____

Address _____

Date Purchased _____Cost_____

Historical Information _____

_____

_____

_____

_____

_____

_____

_____

_____

Item _____

Pattern _____ Size _____

Color Scheme _____

Reference _____

Fabrics & Yardage _____

_____

_____

Completed Cost _____

Date Started _____ Completed _____

PHOTO

Cont'd on next page

Constructed By _____

Quilted By _____

Appraised By _____ Value _____

Updated Appraisals _____ , _____ ; _____ , _____ ; _____ , _____ .
                    Date   Amount   Date   Amount   Date   Amount

Purpose of Project:

Gift   _____
                              Presented to

Sale   _____
                              Sold To

Personal Use _____
                              Used For

Purchased Quilts

Purchased From _____

Address   _____

Date Purchased _____Cost_____

Historical Information _____

_____

_____

_____

_____

_____

_____

_____

_____

_____

Page (   )

PHOTO

Item _____

Pattern _____ Size _____

Color Scheme _____

Reference _____

Fabrics & Yardage _____

_____

_____

Completed Cost _____

Date Started _____ Completed _____

Cont'd on next page

Constructed By _____

Quilted By _____

Appraised By _____ Value _____

Updated Appraisals _____ , _____ ; _____ , _____ ; _____ , _____ .
                    Date   Amount   Date   Amount   Date   Amount

Purpose of Project:

Gift _____
                       Presented to

Sale _____
                       Sold To

Personal Use _____
                       Used For

Purchased Quilts

Purchased From _____

Address _____

Date Purchased _____ Cost _____

Historical Information _____

_____

_____

_____

_____

_____

_____

_____

_____

Item _____

Pattern _____ Size _____

Color Scheme _____

Reference _____

Fabrics & Yardage _____

_____

_____

Completed Cost _____

Date Started _____ Completed _____

PHOTO

Cont'd on next page

Page (   )

Constructed By _____

Quilted By _____

Appraised By _____ Value _____

Updated Appraisals _____ , _____ ; _____ , _____ ; _____ , _____ .
                         Date   Amount   Date   Amount   Date   Amount

Purpose of Project:

Gift _____
                              Presented to

Sale _____
                              Sold To

Personal Use _____
                              Used For

Purchased Quilts

Purchased From _____

Address _____

Date Purchased _____Cost_____

Historical Information _____

_____

_____

_____

_____

_____

_____

_____

_____

PHOTO

Item _____

Pattern _____ Size _____

Color Scheme _____

Reference _____

Fabrics & Yardage _____

_____

_____

Completed Cost _____

Date Started _____ Completed _____

Cont'd on next page

Constructed By _____

Quilted By _____

Appraised By _____ Value _____

Updated Appraisals _____ , _____ ; _____ , _____ ; _____ , _____ .
                   Date   Amount   Date   Amount   Date   Amount

Purpose of Project:

Gift _____
                              Presented to

Sale _____
                               Sold To

Personal Use _____
                              Used For

Purchased Quilts

Purchased From _____

Address _____

Date Purchased _____Cost_____

Historical Information _____

_____

_____

_____

_____

_____

_____

_____

_____

Item _____

Pattern _____ Size _____

Color Scheme _____

Reference _____

Fabrics & Yardage _____

_____

_____

Completed Cost _____

Date Started _____ Completed _____

PHOTO

Cont'd on next page

Constructed By _____

Quilted By _____

Appraised By _____ Value _____

Updated Appraisals _____ , _____ ; _____ , _____ ; _____ , _____ .
                          Date   Amount   Date   Amount   Date   Amount

Purpose of Project:

Gift _____
                          Presented to

Sale _____
                          Sold To

Personal Use _____
                          Used For

Purchased Quilts

Purchased From _____

Address _____

Date Purchased _____Cost_____

Historical Information _____

_____

_____

_____

_____

_____

_____

_____

_____